Haul-Out

Drawings by Marilyn Lemon and
Ann Mikolowski

Foreword by Daniel Hughes

Haul-Out

New and Selected Poems

S<small>TEPHEN</small> T<small>UDOR</small>

Wayne State University Press

Great Lakes Books

A complete listing of the books in this series can be found at the back of this volume.

Philip P. Mason, Editor
Department of History, Wayne State University

Dr. Charles K. Hyde, Associate Editor
Department of History, Wayne State University

Acknowledgments

"Haul Out" and "Season's End" appeared in *The Bridge* 5, no. 2 (Winter 1996); a version of "Queen Anne's Lace" appeared in *Decodings: A Newsletter for the Society of Literature & Science*, Winter 1994.

99 98 97 96   5 4 3 2 1

Library of Congress Cataloging-in-Publication Data

Tudor, Stephen, 1933-
    Haul-out : new and selected poems / Stephen Tudor ; drawings by
Marilyn Lemon and Ann Mikolowski ; foreword by Daniel Hughes.
      p. cm.
    ISBN 0-8143-2659-5 (pbk. : alk. paper)
    1. Great Lakes—Poetry. 2. Sailing—Poetry. I. Title.
PS3570.U37H38   1997
811'.54—dc20   96-21365

Cover and title page photo: Steve Tudor sailing in Georgian Bay with Michael, Tamra, Alex, and Lois. Photo courtesy of Alex Ramos.

Inscription for a Cenotaph

Upriver, through the narrows,

to sail on an inland sea,

lost to us, our Lycidas,

loose in the lake he loved.

Care for him, you Naiads,

if such there be.

—David Herreshoff, 1994

Contents

HAUL-OUT

Part One

Part Two

Part Three

From **HANGDOG REEF**

Foreword

DANIEL HUGHES

In "Falling Overboard for You," Steve Tudor wrote:

> I really didn't see it coming--if I had
> it wouldn't have. First thing I know
> I'm in mid air, sea boots, wet gear,
> twisting, reaching, glimpsing you at
> the taffrail--receding fast.

But this time the speaker will not drown:

> But no, I think, not this time,
> kicking to the surface. Already the
> clouds lifting, an hour to sunset,
> already reassurances: I'm not drowning,
> this is perfectly normal, we're both o.k.

When Steve Tudor lost his life sailing on the Great Lakes in 1994, his friends and readers knew it would not be "o.k." and that the "reassurances" would probably never come. But the poems he left behind, so splendidly gathered in this volume, give us a solace and a memory and remind us, in the words of Wallace Stevens, how poetry helps us to live our lives.

This book, which includes the best poems from the earlier *Hangdog Reef*, shows a poet moving from the physical to the metaphysical, from the descriptive to the symbolic, without ever losing the precise detail and the witty observations that informed his poetry from the beginning. Nor are all the poems in this book about sailing. Wonderful flower poems like "Bouquet" and "Japanese Honeysuckle" show the same descriptive gifts as the sailing poems, but in these works, the poet manifests a different intimacy and a further transformation.

From "Japanese Honeysuckle":

> There is our strength,
>
> in the daft flowering and seed-shed,
>
> the grip and terrifying curl,
>
> the frantic envelopment.

From "Bouquet":

> not stems elegant in their thorns and crisp skins,
>
> but just a bit of the ordinary
>
> and you're not to keep them, not to enshrine them
>
> there in your room, there in your crystal,
>
> but maybe you'll smile--see how shameless I am--
>
> maybe you'll smile and say, "orchids, orchids from
>
> Paris."

Yet it is, of course, the sailing poems that constitute Steve Tudor's unique achievement. Because he is no longer with us, it is tempting to overemphasize the deep elegiac note in his work, but the archetype of the doomed sailor-poet is irresistible. We do not think of the drowned Hart Crane or Shelley as victims of accident, but rather as fulfillers of their destinies. Crane's "Voyages" poems and Shelley's "Adonais" are unquestionable prefigurations of their shortened lives. The sailor-poet tempts the cruel muses; he lives near the beginning of things, and he courts their end as well. But this elegiac impulse in Tudor is both resisted and embraced. In his beautiful elegy for a young woman, "Mask Maker," we see the double impulse:

> I want to link up with you somewhere,
> Toronto, Key West, not just talk to
> you in stupid, elegiac tones. My plan was
> to marry you from the time you were five
> and us run off to beautiful Bend, Oregon,
> or coastal Maine. Can't you rise from
> your ashes, take wing like the grown
> woman you are and you and me go fishing
> and build a fire and cook those always
> brainless bluegills? Wherever you are
> I believe that matter's indestructible,
> that creation reverses entropy and that
> you remain splendid in your outrageous
> dress, your plain words, your proud eye.

The doomed sailor-poet cannot escape his fate, perhaps, but we must not ignore the intense pleasure and clarifying insight that sailing gives him, and through him, his readers. From "Sailing Vision":

> It's as if you could see across the lake,
> sixty, a hundred miles, across its curved
> and breathing shoulder, your eyesight has
> so unexpectedly improved.

The external voyage becomes an inner one, and the poet discovers words as well as water:

> And this you bring back: the hours
> before sunrise, loneliness that puts you
> in touch, the wordless moment
> that makes all language possible.

Perhaps the central lament in these poems is that you can't be sailing *all the time*. Sailing is the New, Motion, Delight in Mastery and Purpose. It is impossible that it should ever stop. "Haul-Out," in which that sailor-poet must put up his boat for the winter, is another elegy, but fortified by Tudor's unique tone of regret and resistance as man and boat become one:

> It's only my life, this banged up, obsolete
> plastic heap with its faded gelcoat, frayed lines
> and . . . poor me. And we'd engaged so intensely,
> skin, hair, teeth, nails, the roots of the flesh,
> it barely seemed I'd the strength to make it
> Bristol, and now it's come time for hanging it up,
> tanks cleared, engine drained, compartments
> left open to air, and then the canvas
> to tent us against the impossible weather.

Steve Tudor came upon his impossible weather, but the existence of these bracing poems makes us feel, in an ironic yet strengthening way, that he survived it.

Haul-Out

Part One

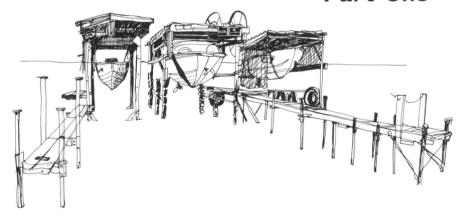

Good Wind

All day long the good wind
but you are stuck at home—
Trees express it in their
slow, serious choreography and hushed
     music.
Gulls scale the invisible altitudes
in their anguish and crowding hunger,
downcurving at last to lakelevel.
Early on, at the seawall, the envy:
five sloops walking up river and into
the clad chest of the lake—
so full of themselves in their sailsuits
     and heeling moment
you could have blanketed them each
with a spelled and vacuous curse—
Go.
Let the sadness disperse
in the spoon and arched cup of the sky.

Overnight Solo, Lake St. Clair

Gusting along in the small hours,
and town's off across the waves
to the southwest, towers lit with
the refractions of mopping crews
and someone's late intellectual fire.

I'm freezing, and have on, as well
as long-johns, two hooded coats,
work gloves and a woolen cap equipped
with flaps and chin strings, and
what with the waves being so rude

it's much busier managing than I'd
guessed. Wasn't travel by water
a leisure activity? Sea air, good
food, a healthful ride on the way
to some inviting and reassuringly dry

place? Though the stars make themselves
apparent through the mists overhead,
these are the memories I'll keep:
the drive through darkness to the
last buoy, the turn, the road home.

Trade: Lake Erie

Sailing back at night
   a bulk carrier lights up
      to make sure we see it coming,

a larger, many tapered town,
   dark, diagonal.
      I cannot sleep

for that sleepless,
   reverberating toil.
      Wheat, copper,

limestone, scrap iron,
   our own predation.
      Thoughtful

to fire up like that.
   We put one another
      quickly abaft

though in that early,
   absent hour
      neither boat seems to move.

To an Old Laker

Say you're in service fifty years.
Finally the ship-breakers take you—
Spain, Brazil, Korea. Not under
your own power, but you're towed

then torched: cut up for scrap.
New ships rise upon your ashes,
but what possible consolation,
that we dozed in the star-cold

graves of our bunks to your long
rhythms, walked your wordless decks,
watched the eloquent shore slide by
a life or two of seasons—

Or we'll read in the *Free Press*
that the tow cut loose near the
Azores or seven hundred miles off
Seattle, the tug itself a junker.

You rolled, gradually filled. All
our inventions follow from devastation,
launch, undergo trials, set out in
the clear and breathing eye of the day.

The Wreck in the Cove at Great Duck Island

The long shape just below the surface
in such clear water. Rowing the length of it
(double planked, ribs exposed, deck gone),
calls to mind other coves across the lakes
where crews just managed to bring vessels in,
seams parted, rudders broken, shafts bent
from bottoming out in troughs close to shore.

Now the light's automated no one puts in here.
Storms gravel the landing; and when we walk
the track to the station we notice creatures
unafraid in their solitude: a pair of marsh
hawks, wood chucks, a badger, an opossum, a
    world
on its own among willows and in birches and
conifers higher up and over the ridge to

the two empty houses with their ruined gardens,
children's sand box, sheds and pump house,
and beyond them, at water's edge, the light
in its white-painted conical tower and flanking,
thick-walled Canada Coast Guard building.
So many clues to the life that was: walks,
bird feeder, clothes line, stacked fire wood,

impromptu signs painted on boards nailed to trees.
We rest for a time near sections of a tower
that once sent radio beacons across the lakes.
God or someone—the joke's on us—has decamped,
and the hawks glide at our shoulders with fierce
cries, the pair of them, wings darkening the sky
in their hunger for their own solitude returned.

The Winnipeg Aground

1.

Looking down river from our park
the Winnipeg aground where
the ship channel skirts Belle Isle.

Five tugs try to free her—she took
the turn wide at an unlighted can
downbound from Duluth, at night, in fog.

Day and night I pace the seawall,
binoculars suspended from my neck,
hand-held VHS tuned in—the voice

of the skipper—he hasn't slept—
the bridges of the tugs—a coast guard
vessel, methodical, taking soundings.

2.

I take no pleasure in her grief,
deck and running lights ablaze,
engines full ahead to assist the

tugs straining at their warps or,
nose to her bow, pushing to free her
from the suction of fine blue clay.
Thirty-six hours, and the diesels

are no match for the clay, not an inch
forward for all their labor.

She's laden with grain, product of
Manitoba, Alberta, Saskatchewan,
miles of it shipped east by rail

and the cars flipped over hoppers,
the grain elevated, sent cascading
through chutes into the ship.

3.

Day three, the company relieves the
skipper, calls in a lighter. He's sure
to suffer harm: his command, his career.

Not one of us in small craft but have
touched bottom where rivers shallow
or where gravel or limestone forms

ridges in a shoulder of a lake.
The Coast Guard had pulled the lighted
buoys above Belle Isle for the season

the day before Winnipeg grounded;
her pilot or steersman had noticed
too late and made the turn too late.
And now a barge with crane and bucket
ties to her side, and the lighter
(the stripped hulk of a vessel) alongside.

4.

. . . two-and-a-half days to off-load
the grain from the Canadian prairie,
so much of it to transfer in order

to float her, grain spilled onto
decks, into currents, in my glasses
I could see it, tawny, drifting

from the bucket, lights glaring,
the clank and grind of machinery
wafting across the dark mile of river.

She'd pop free any time, but when
it happened I was home—asleep in my bed
and by that next morning she'd sailed,

lighter, barge too, and winter took
the river then, the days darker, yellowed
grass at the seawall, gulls, a stillness.

De Tour Reef Light

1.

Always a trip crossing Lake Huron,
marking the reef light from miles off shore—
squat white tower on a masonry base

the weather can't budge. Seen from
down lake it fades in and out as
a bluish nub in the haze where

water and sky meet, then, as you
close, the contours of the land
resolve and the shaft stands clear—

mark where oreboats make the turn
past Drummond, past De Tour Village,
up the St. Marys to Soo locks.

2.

Looking south from the village
the upbound vessels show first
as smoke plumes against the horizon,

then their fore and aft deck houses,
then the black hulls appear. Transiting
docks, ferry landing and "Fogcutter" bar

they give us a look—their names,
hailing ports, flags and stack colors.
In ballast, summer in their lines,
even so they anticipate November,
ice forming on decks, storms,
darkness, and then the shutting down.

Atomic Four

But it's only an ailing, elderly, in-line four—
I tenderly haul it, halyard to lifting ring,
tote it to basement, warm it, sponge its brow.
The pan's not been off since 'seventy-two; I've
broken it down before, but with head removed

inspection reveals a further build-up of carbon,
time worn rings, valves that require grinding,
reseating. Old thing, you'll be happy to know
your guides are still true, and your bearings,
they'll do but for one and four on the crank,

which I'll have to replace. How still you lie
in your long travail and inner parts revealed.
Language endures; you too in your eloquent
   trope
outwit the seasons but for simple neglect or
changes of heart. I'll time you, gap you, fit

you with fresh gaskets, cap, plugs and impeller.
Try dreaming up sonnets; listen closely to how
words achieve music in clear air up the lakes.
Sing to yourself and grow strong. I'll bed you,
align you, trust you to bear off the lee shore.

Paul Bunyan, Keweenaw Peninsula

If only with my own two hands I could wrench
these enormous trees up—just to give the world
something to remember. But where should I stack them
for safe keeping? Or should I merely burn them?

I want to ravage a mountain, the Porkies, anywhere,
attack it with bars, decimate it with gunpowder,
and where that mountain stood I'd set a field of stones,
desolate, hard-edged, impossible to traverse and

so vast that to comprehend it they'd have to
manufacture a tower. I want to lay down thick, many-
stranded cables, terrible in their strength,
connectors to bed rock, dams, stadiums.

And if God allowed me to have my way, all my
stacks, my conflagrations, stone fields and rough
spun wire ropes would express an uncouth, jagged,
barely detectable but unmistakable symmetry, as when

a sprawl of rough, lichen-covered boulders in some arid,
neglected back land is discovered to have pattern and
human intent, or as when the wind and rain against
window panes metamorphose to a song, a painting, a
    poem.

ANN VROBLOWSKI

Sailing Vision

It's as if you could see across the lake,
sixty, a hundred miles, across its curved
and breathing shoulder, your eyesight has
so unexpectedly improved.

And never mind the capes and haunting inlets,
you steer by clouds and the hunches of birds,
every slippery, gliding, breathing thing.

And this you bring back: the hours
before sunrise, loneliness that puts you
in touch, the wordless moment
that makes all language possible.

The Gott Locks Through

Sault Ste. Marie

From where we're holding place in the approach
we see her topsides rise against the sky
with the grave measure of seasons, crops, clocks—
I wonder what to match it to—stars, then,
but still it's only machines shrewdly managed
to allow for water hoisting her. Our turn's
next, and we'll ride the influx to the top
looking, for the benefit of the locksmen,
as practiced as we possibly can—we'd fit
handily into one of the Gott's hip pockets.

My crew controls bow and stern lines to hold
us fast against the upswell as we climb.
Can't help but think "this is Superior,"
the big lake in its flood and freeze and praise
filling the Poe as a kind of afterthought
in its calm run to Huron. Crowds wave to us
from the observation deck. For once it's us,
our images that will liven snaps and videos
coast to coast, perhaps because we wave back,
life in the eye, light locked into itself.

The Gott, meanwhile, steams patiently upstream:
as far as the reef light the channel's tight,
then comes Whitefish Bay, then the lake makes
    room,

so much of it that even she may feel
lost, or at least lonesome. Hey, stay in touch,
we want to tell her, but she's a town, a state
unto herself, and it's more *us* we mean,
along with gulls and trees and petroglyphs:
we'll be the lonely ones in our provident
steps up the scarcely sheltered east shore.

The oreboats, they steam onwards unperturbed,
that's their charm, though they too may hole
   and sink,
thousand foot or no—and when they go the lake
cloaks them the same with an indifferent wave,
and more than us they take the generations
with them in each voice that cries out to us
as we relive their going down. But we,
when our time comes, no one remembers us.
Small craft live or die by their wits and that's
our pride, the way we earn our solitude.

Part Two

HANGDOG REEF

HORIZON FOR PAUL   Ann Mikolowski

Beach Find, North Channel

"Look around you"

Darch Island, the bleached cow's skull
   at water's edge, orbits hollow
where the luminous eyes took in
   summer and sunsets, gnats dancing
in thinnish light. We spotted it there
   tilted into grey, skin-smooth stones,
the eloquent tongue vanished in its
   hungers and music, the horns
nipped or somehow rotted away.
   Sad beast, bellowing pasture poet,
of all mother images the mother
   gazing reproachfully across the fence,
green grass, the rain falling,
   waves all day lapping the shingle:
you have become your own monument, staring
   into nothing, priding yourself in silence.

Agawa Rock: Lake Superior

In my prized world you and I cruise north.
Can't say how long we make it last—days?
weeks? We'd plan ahead. But I picture
the time we reach our farthest point out,
some remote cove, Superior, rock bound,
and not a dock or road within miles.

Settling into that wilderness we'd practice
the entire alphabet of tongues it is
so still and alone, but even there
on that far, sad, wet, shimmering beach
there would be signs of our other lives
tossed up by storms or gradually edging in:

sawn wood on small, provident waves, glass,
plastic—not much, and what there is
transformed by the work of the elements,
bleached, purified from what they were,
and then we would be moved to remember:
our names, our jobs, the day and the date.

And at night, rocking in our moored
berths and breathing skin, I see us choosing:
we don't belong here, let's go back home,
this is no Eden. Next morning, even as we
hoist anchor and leave the cove behind
deer make their way to the water's edge.

Shingle Beach, Lake Superior Provincial Park

Large, coarse, waterworn gravel:
I want to make a poem from this,
how looking into such slopes at
lake edge you look back into time,
shales from the Upper Devonian that
tend to flats and ovals; whitish,
irregular fragments of limestone;
cobbles of pink-flecked granite,
slick black basalt in broken lumps.

Some resonate when struck or make
a music when you stir them with
your boot; it's as if they protested
too much. Did not believe you gave
offense but sang to show mere stone,
if challenged, could liberate the
chimes that lie at the heart of
things. To look into such stones

is to look into fire's infinite
selves where the surrounding
darkness denies and affirms. And your
anguish at stars, and the moon's
unrequited desire, and your own,
pale bones in their whispering
marrow respond to the timbres of

rock—so that when you turn away
and without looking back take the
path to the road you're renewed,
linked once more to the igneous
depths of earth, that glowing plane
and fiery center that lies beneath
and beyond the ancient roots.

Sinclair Cove

More like a cave with its granite wall and
boulder jumble. You pick your way in through
islands of the smooth, reddish stone—safe

against the surge. What's this history mean—
our personal ventures, lives of the peoples
who made the drawings on rock, the records

left us in sediments, erosion, rift and uplift?
You tie your boat to the last solid section
of ruined pier—weathered planking, rusted

bolts, stone ballast. Someone appears to be
listening, carefully, to test your intentions:
"do what you will, you're on your own." So cool

the air to breathe you sleep into the depths of
clear water, beach timber and trails patiently
stepping into the brush. Some day that good,

ineluctable silence will prevail. We ourselves
will go into darkness. Earth will again become
itself, meaningless, lonely, utterly at peace.

Rattlesnake Harbor

"THE 'DOUBLE NATURED' ASPECT
    OF THE PHENOMENAL WORLD"

This limestone with its whitish
ledges of layered sea creatures moves
you and me to explore our pasts together,
nails and hair, shell whorl, sea worm,

all of us, and the water's so clear
with the iron and ship's timbers down there
the fish will only bite if we look away from them—
if you look my way and I look yours.

               Wash my face
and teach me the instress of loons,
the double nature of coalinths
bedded in the fragments I found this morning,
rock shelving into baskets of years,
shapes saved for the future.

Snowbound, Skull Island

The clouds were scattered pages,
  sad novels, yellowed newsprint.
My arm was an axe with an edge.
  All day birds telephoned south.
Their voices sounded far away,
  drowning, maybe, in blue-black floes.
My stove boat locked into the ice
  like a grieving heart in its chest.
I built a shelter of bark and loneliness,
  the roof tree was a tolling bell,
the hearth glowed and died
  like a star falling through Cassiopeia.
To sail away in the spring was a
  promise of distance and hunger.
Winter fitted me in skins, took me,
  covered my head. Such a silence—
provisions, traps and snares,
  the constant looking into ashes.

Singlehander, Lake Huron, 1992

". . . YOU MAY BE THE RUIN OF US BOTH."

—VENUS TO ADONIS, *METAMORPHOSIS*

Not bad duty, lying here with my
head in her lap as she regales me
with tall tales and devouring advice.

And I'm going back out there tonight
even though she argues against it
as bothersome if not slightly fatal.

It's the lonesomeness I dread most
booming along the course, and my
own cooking, which is less than zip.

Otherwise, let her swan away; if
something bad happens she'll only say
I told you, stay out of the woods.

Thanks, Venus. You do more for me
than harnesses and jack lines. Thanks
Venus, from the bottom of the night.

Falling Overboard for You

I really didn't see it coming—if I had
it wouldn't have. First thing I know
I'm in mid air, sea boots, wet gear,
twisting, reaching, glimpsing you at
the taffrail—receding fast.

What I did to deserve this was
ignore a frayed painter
lowering the dinghy into the current.
Pop went the line, me plunging in to port,
water closing over.

But no, I think, not this time,
kicking to the surface. Already the
clouds lifting, an hour to sunset,
already reassurances: I'm not drowning,
this is perfectly normal, we're both o.k.

Blue Water Bridge

Like the time I came back from up north,
seven weeks: North Channel, Georgian Bay,
passing under the bridge deck was the
end of it, how the truck tires pounded,

how currents ripped and twisted the boat,
the entire lake emptying out there,
past chemical valley—Canada—
past downtown Port Huron—the U.S.—

eyes fried, skin desiccated, nails chopped.
Why come back just to put on a tie
and punch clock? And on a Sunday, a load
of stinkboats, wakes you wouldn't believe,

wind flukey, dropping to nothing five
miles from the range, and a hatch of flies,
biters, me aiming for the seven
sisters, grieving, marking the last miles home.

Saturday Morning

My protoganglia to yours—
your soma, your flesh, your tissues,
your hypothalamus, liver, endocrine gland, pancreas,
your lymph system, alimentary canal, eustachian tubes,
all those in me speaking to all those in you,

my ur-self to your ur-self,
my molecules to yours, our cell-mitosis, our
inter-connecting de-oxy-ribonucleic acids,
transmitters, twined, encoded, splitting,
recombining in us across hours, across miles.

That's how we take flight, and last night, too,
with the desperate moon in its net of wind.

Wind Vane

Ebony arrow on a stalk atop the spar—
so sensitive in your jeweled bearing
yet strong to withstand plunging

and heavy air. It's with such care
that I mount you, aim, set tabs and
torque you down: you're very nearly

unapproachable there at the masthead
and when and if you do fall to the gale
may my own sense of the invisible

approximate yours, wind in my hair,
breeze at my back, points of the compass
bred in the bone, true to life as yours.

Not Allowed to Anchor

One of my best stops, De Tour Village,
and the Department of Natural Resources,

with its gas dock, pump-out and wired,
watered slips, has a lock on the harbor.

What's a poet to do, who can't set flukes,
fall off to a suitable length, cleat down

and call it a day? Such a pleasure
to take the dinghy ashore, walk up town,

savor the houses, the faces, the prospect
of the squat, black and white ferry

chugging back and forth between the mainland
and Drummond Island (strolling to the Fogcutter

for a beer and a burger). How spoiled I was
back when. No dock, no dock master, no order

to move out or else. I'm my own worst enemy
to look back to the days before progress.

Boatspeed

I complain how in light air my old
boat doesn't point high—

hull designed to an old rule,
generous underbody, long keel,
rig that limits its sailplan.

I've done all I can think of,
never mind the furling,
the extras I carry.

But the new designs, every point,
they outperform—

Remember how I stood proud.
Waves broke across the bow.
The sun burned fiercely.
I sailed to every corner of the lakes.

Haul-Out

It's haul-out day, later in the season
than is good for the boat or me. I rig
a gin pole, tie halyards and stays back
and pull the mast, careful not to smash
antenna or vane coming down. Snow flurries,
glazes on puddles, this is the month of storms,
vessels iced-over at mid-lake. Sure I give
thanks for the luck I've had, for you
especially; for summer and sunlight, and
there she hangs in her slings. I raise her,
take a brush to her, cleanse her of algae and
sediments, wash away my own season's sins.

It's only my life, this banged up, obsolete
plastic heap with its faded gelcoat, frayed lines
and . . . poor me. And we'd engaged so intensely,
skin, hair, teeth, nails, the roots of the flesh,
it barely seemed I'd the strength to make it
Bristol, and now it's come time for hanging it up,
tanks cleared, engine drained, compartments
left open to air, and then the canvas
to tent us against the impossible weather.

Part Three

Pajamas

three a.m. coming downstairs,
sitting at a table in the darkness
not listening, not thinking,

letting the chill enter your body,
your bare feet, shoulders, temples,
muscles growing stiff, water in

a glass, and the next you know
you're back in bed (climbed the
stairs blind), and you've crossed

your hands, formal, on your chest,
head centered on pillow, then,
sinking, you turn on your side . . .

Steam Radiators

It's an old house and they whisper
and they hiss and it's as if someone
were speaking who smoked three packs
a day, had a chest condition and,
in his imperfect memory for names
kept wheezing "who . . . was . . . it, what . . .
was . . . he . . . called?" And this is late
and it's dark out but for streetlights
and my face reflects in the window,
here, beside my desk, in the sunroom
that I've made my study— An old
"mushroom" steam boiler-conversion
that used to be coal-fired, down there
in the basement, and it's gone on
doing its job. . . . And when those iron
radiators are silent I hear the low,
sustained rumble of truck and auto
traffic which is the city's night song,
a little snow in the streets, ice in
the canal, and I hear clocks ticking
all through the house, it's that quiet,
and if I were to slump over in my chair
and die right now I'd already be home.

Sun Burn

The birds of the sun eat flesh:
first the backs of hands, the
foreheads, ears, feet. This is
solitude; and to know the wind rush,
the darkness, the storms making a
harp of lines is to lie sleepless,
gripping, ungripping the body
in its tripped equilibrium and
repositioning thirst. "What will
become of me?" Wide awake so
early it's nowhere in the calendar,
living that one lonesome memory,
a double rainbow at Rogers City,
image astride the wall, brief, the
center blazing, the cry of grief.

Loud Noise

About three houses down, a loud bang
and we sit up in bed in our wild hair
and unfocused eyes. It's in our minds,
I want to say, something wild, that
soldiers have dragged our neighbor from
his rooms, shot him on his front lawn.
Looking out our window, the cold pane,
nothing stirs in our street except
the moonlight in its leisurely traverse
and in that blue, charismal light we
can see other curtains drawn back
and still no movement in the street or
further sound, not a cat prowling, not
one leaf skittering from a tree. What
are we to make of this unlooked for
explosion? The sound of it echoes,
everywhere, and everywhere there are
faces at windows, perplexed, a curtain
drawn back, for once, from the night.

Left and Right Handed

All right, miracles of
   dexterity, sensitivity,
strength, expressiveness. . . .
   Human history in its gardens
grows enough of you.
   Whoever troubled to invent
rings, bracelets, nail polish?

Take my own
   gripping a swing's chains
or flipping pages.
   Better yet counting money.
They have their life—
   I have mine, except
that I for one am unattached.

Picture the "praying hands,"
   how they gave themselves
to benefit their pal—who was
   the one who made the drawing.
My own hands—they have their own
   objections even as they
tap, tap, tap these words out.

Even now they try to come to
   grips with themselves,
the left with its gold ring,
   the right with its childhood scar.
What does the world tell us?
   What will happen to us
with all our skills and ten fingers?

Losing a Poem to the Screen

Confused I shut the power down
where I meant to save.
All those bluish, faint tracks
against a green, backlit ground—

Vanished. So many dying embers,
so many wanton schoolboys
breaking ranks,
scurrying into the dark.

Tempting, isn't it, to liken this loss
to our own hearts and minds
flickering out
as if by some accident of fate
on an ordinary day.

And time stretches on without us,
the apples we loved (golden delicious),
our shapes curled together on a bed,
our hats on a nail—

I rush back to the keyboard.
Scattered phrases, images,
the closing sentence,
I punch in everything I can remember:
save this poem, this penitent life!

Creosote Curiosity

The roof's leaking at the chimney;
I drag out the ladder, haul up the
tar and paddle from the hardware store.

It's a sure thing I'll come down
with black goo on my hands, face,
shirt and shoes. I love the smell.

Easy to the porch roof, but the pitch
to the peak scares me. I follow up a
valley, fingers raw with shingle grit.

And there I am, straddling the peak
beside the weathered, reassuring brick
of the uncapped chimney with its

sprung, antediluvian tv antenna
angling off to the north. What a view.
Tree tops, roof tops, back yards,

I can see into my neighbor's upstairs
windows! Just don't look down, as
they say. Just slob the creosote on

above and below the flashing, reaching
around, stretching, braving the heady
air, this summit of your handyman's

ambition, before it's too late, before
the cold wind blows, and it all
comes down, chimney, walls, everything.

Bouquet

Darling, here's a bit of grass
pulled from a waste place behind my building.
Here's some gum weed, some sow thistle, some wild
    lettuce . . .
snake root, common fleabane, all from the edge of
    the road.

And it's a hot day and these poor things,
already they're less than fresh,
they're tough but they're tired, didn't expect
that I'd come along and tear them up for you.

Not even a knife or a sharp pair of scissors,
but just torn up by the roots, clumped together
and thrust into a paper.
Darling, here's a bit of grass, some thin, twisted
    things

for you, to show how I love you, and no
they're not roses, not fragrant petals floating in a
    bowl,
not stems elegant in their thorns and crisp skins,
but just a bit of the ordinary

and you're not to keep them, not to enshrine them
there in your room, there in your crystal,
but maybe you'll smile—see how shameless I am—
maybe you'll smile and say, "orchids, orchids from
    Paris."

Spotted Touch-Me-Not

FOR ADRIANA KERBER

Going back, say, to *An American in Paris*,
Gene Kelly and Lesley Caron, you remembered:
the orange-gold petals with their red-
brown patches, the curious, sharply spurred
sac, the capsule that exploded when touched,
spiraling out its small, insistent seeds.

Life imitates art. The music, pictures and
books we read dated so fast. But wildflowers,

they're on the long cycle, and for them,
fashion's no bar. You knew where they grew,
Touch-me-nots along the chain link fence,
clumps of the succulent, translucent stems,
and you pointed them out in an illumination
from childhood, and nothing had changed

but we too might give ourselves at a touch
to the blue, unimpeachable riverine world.

Japanese Honeysuckle

FOR JENNIFER MCGLAUCHLIN

        Go. It's not
bad to immerse yourself in your life.

See how the five slender stamens curve
gracefully to their beige powdery tips.
In among them, the willowy style offers

its lemon-colored stigma with the certitude
of moonlight fallen on streams. No one

truly belongs. We're all imports escaped from
gardens, as alone as stars in their

diamond space. Nip the corolla's base,
draw the nectar: it's a wine that
returns children to the winged music of trees.

There is our strength,
in the daft flowering and seed-shed,
the grip and terrifying curl,
the frantic envelopment.

Bedstraw

galium verum

Is it any wonder that the extremely fine
airy, green-yellow clusters, articulate
as arpeggios, sing to us in the morning?

Any wonder that the five
lanciolate leaf spikes at the nodes, where
stems divide and redivide, ever slenderer,
to a tracery as of sprawled or flung stars,
call to us quietly?

And all for pallets or pillows,
that grows near streams weak-stemmed,
leaning against bushes, pliant, sweet-smelling.
Somehow I am so late to this courage,
this mute eloquence, the silhouette crisp,
that speaks to the selves of me in the face
of bedlam, endless temporizing, limbs aghast.

Pigweed

Why haven't I one tenth the genius
of Ludwig B.? Yesterday I appeared
on the radio and it was any weather
you can name, but I thrive in disturbed
ground and dry and without song—so
long as my own loneliness escapes me,
and that, the people admired.

      A hundredth of his
genius—I that am axial and terminal
flowering, a limp-leafed thing beside
the road with rough, hairy stem,
likewise but too infrequently called
Green Amaranth.

      The announcer said
whose namesake are you? My voice shook
to its root; I wanted to tell him half
brother to Narcissus by the nymph Clovia,
my cousins the Everlastings never fade,
we're Immortals to poets . . .

      Pigweed. Each
has his better self if only the stars
knew and understood us. Just now, the
Sonata in G Major, *adagio grazioso,*

and I'm at home, I die, it's where I live,
mute beast, inexpressible soul, weed
without talent, agent of allergies, heavy
shouldered, shame-faced crier to heaven.

Queen Anne's Lace

Brush Ford Park

The Year They Didn't Mow

These flat-topped clusters of tiny
    cream-white blossoms with one dark,
        reddish brown floret usually at the center

float at knee level, thigh level,
    clouds of them beside summer paths through
    grass,
        nodding as you pass, whispering at your
    pantleg,

that open and acknowledge from an incurled
    palm,
        the pale taproot and father of carrots
            gripping down through turf, topsoil, clay

to rock marrow, joint and earth nerve:
    from a single embryonic cell in tissue culture
        they have resurrected, flowered, seeded,

even to that rust floret—
    such is love, the half-conscious drift of it,
        the current and deep strength of it.

Artichokes, Little Bay de Noc

"SERVE ONE TO EACH DINER. THE LEAVES ARE
DIPPED, ONE AT A TIME, IN A SAUCE AND
THE LOWER END IS SIMPLY PULLED THROUGH
THE TEETH TO EXTRACT THE TENDER EDIBLE
PORTION. THE LEAF IS THEN DISCARDED."

My extreme privacy—my heart.
You'd savor each of them,
the fleshy bases of the leaves,
the artichoke disrobed, taking
a week if you wished,
drawing me to you tooth and tongue
until the heart lay bare.

What then of me stripped but the
sum of my responses—unless you
shadowed me into myself
and every step I took you took
so that I no longer grieved
but joined you, tender seed,
piquant flavor, moist portion—

joined you to the singular me not yet
stickery thistle. But this is madness.
Even as I open to you I sorrow.
You may take and go, you may stay,
I'll be the more alone for it tomorrow.

Writing

four poems in one sitting, think of
Motor City Salvage, ice boxes, stoves,
flivers rusting under the snow, junk
steel, masses of tires, the cheerful
scampering rats in their rat families—
how all this took years, manufacturing,
distribution, purchase, use, throwing
out, all that like words evolving from
their grunts and hisses into eloquence,
and still later their gradual disuse,
their oblivion in lost orations, and
thinking of this as the history of murder
how can four poems in one sitting make
it? They would be so thin we'd take
them for the ghosts of stoves, ice
boxes, vans and rats, even though as
we held them in our hands they'd
stain us with their rust, tears and
sweat, cry out to us: *accept us for*
what we are, a moment's inspiration,
a thought so fragile the poet barely
netted us as we settled momentarily
on the blue vase or calyx, flower
nodding in wind, wings beating slow.

Comet

It's November, 6:30 in the morning,
cold, stars vivid from the north wind.

No one's here but for the river
and beyond the river the presence of the lake.
I'm walking the dog in the park.

My child's starbook with its grainy paper,
faded primary colors and frayed pages
described the ellipse comets make,
the power of the sun to sling rock and ice
far out into the solar system

only to have it fall back—
slowly at first, then ever faster
back to that cold solar fury.

A colder wind tests my scarf and cap.
There it hangs southeast over the lake,
30 degrees up, the blurred disk
the misty, curving tail urgent
and indifferent at once,
lonelier than the other stars.

Only you will understand, who taught me
shapes, passionate repetition, requiem
communion, only you in your own segment
of the arc and returning seasons.

Part Four

R. S. Thomas

You struggle against the wind
up the desolate cliff road
below your stone-lonesome chapel.

The universal dampness—there is
no central heating in all Wales—
settles into lungs, sinuses, ears,

slate floors—this is the theology
of discontent, or impatience, or
tired-of-being-stuck-here-ness,

and you kibitz your parishioners
and god and the harmless, bleating
sheep. Certainly, sunlight on a

field you unthinkingly passed by
may have led to a birth into truth;
meanwhile you sit down to porridge,

contemplating the latest in
liturgical fashion which some clown
at Westminster has published

in the *Anglican Herald*. Still,
you know, dear man, how we admire
your courage. You've faced Him

down in His own green sanctuary
where, you tell us, the grasses
bury everything before its time

and the memory of our lives fails
but for depressions in church yards
which say someone once walked here.

A Morning Back

FOR JACK CLEMENTS

. . . CONVENTIONAL GRIEF AND
EXTRAVAGANT ADULATION

—E. M. W. TILLYARD ON DRYDEN'S "ODE TO ANN KILLIGREW"

1. Water

It's taking leave of the mutable regions
below the moon when, loosing the lines,
we sail. In changing, night and day and in
all weathers, the water's constant, a known
compared to the land, and especially now
that the solstice draws us into the earth.

We embark upon another planet. Eloquent
stones wait patiently beneath the surface
to speak to our doubts. At last, questions
surface we did not know troubled our every
day labors, so that the logic of the gulls
resolves itself into patience and hunger.

Towards noon we enter the region of fixed
stars and the great, angelic circle. Only
the highest landforms linger on the round
horizon. Wind itself invades the flesh of
us, constant fragment of the blue, boreal
sky and driver of the ship's round hull.

GHOSTRIDERS   *ANN MIKOLOWSKI*

And later we're farther from earth, having
achieved the empyrean of the one rule and
birthing fire. Our discreet selves, which
hung so tenaciously upon rib and skullbone,
retreat to the hidden places, against the
day, returning, we resume our lives ashore.

2. *Shore*

Lock up the boat, walk away: it sleeps.
You enter tree greenness and the
unfathomable grasses of shore life, oar
to shoulder, rainbow and covenant of
ships lifted away to the stowage of towns.

Strange how thin and active spirits in
the blood (pleasure and knowledge of waves)
disperse in streets. It's as if you grew
thick with macadam and glass, lost touch,
crushed the hollow bones of your ancient

bird's pinions—hoping not to lose
sight of mast and hoist. Inevitably the
road bends. Wings of ripening grain
fold upon you, and soon your own dark
shadow pools at your feet—a morning

back from the beach, an afternoon tripped
among the arcane pilots of highways,
far from sea swell, where the knowledge
of soundings lies cold and the world
goes dry but for its blue, watery eye.

3. *Sun*

Cats, clocks, rich rooms, playgrounds,
roofed markets and church spires: the
sun imagines them. Summers when we sail
we go to school to its local temper;
shadow islands, passages, reefs, dunes,
crouch in the spun needles of its light.
Fastidious and eccentric, the sun sires
melon-flowers, flaming birds, roses,
parakeets and barbaric glass. We favor
the long port tack for its shielding jib
and heat's relief. Clarity of line is
the sun's virtue yet the arc of its
burning relents so that sinking to
darkness over water, glazed, autumnal,
the sun accedes to the long pause and
journey home, the wakening into sleep.

4. *Air*

There are no creatures in all the cloud
bestiary but birth in our eyes, first
as shadows, then as shapes intense as
the hungers they reflect. Then the wind
shifts moods, darkens, opens to another
gallery. Landforms drop astern until mere
shreds of cumulus signal what was underfoot.
Unplumbed and pathless, the sky's a net
of air highways and each fragment's a

country in the four-colored over-arching
atlas of the mind. But all these things
we imagine, even as danger. There is no
storm or cast of irredeemable sorrow or
galling star, but our desires turn upon
us, so that what we've dreamed, we become.

5. *Man*

Seeking out my fathers, nothing's ideal,
not the unmopped deck, sailing out, not
stretched mainsail or worn, tangled line.
My Odyssey's to magnify the prose of me,
expose each vacuity of skin and tilted
verb, confess to the lexicon of skewed
trim and cupped argument, hero despite my
trailing grip and tiller's curved intent.

It's as if the fleet of the world lurked
just beyond the horizon. If I do learn my
name in some island archive—written in
an arcane language in an impossible hand—
time, then, to bear the standard of it
home. Then, at last, crossing those waste
distances, the land or seascape will, one
green-gold day, resolve into the familiar.
Only trees at the entrance will differ.
Walking into the house of my fathers,
nothing and everything will have changed.

Mask Maker

FOR JENNIFER MCGLAUCHLIN

Masks from the Old World—
  mummery, faschnacht,
demons, dominoes, caricatures,
  you loved creating these
discrete selves, these faces
  imposed on faces,
leather, cloth, papier-mâché.
  And costume—you came to
view dress itself as theater
  in the increasingly bold,
bright fabrics you wore,
  in your stage hats,
scarves, powders and paints.
  Such guises—in them
the true, fierce you
  blossomed, grew strong
even as you withdrew.

I don't recall you fell off a swing
and hit your head. Bee stings? First
Boyfriends? You *were* stubborn, and
fought your brother and his buddies
not to be left behind climbing, hiking
summer's island in its woods, marshes,

rockfall and sandy point. What made
you wild escapes me, but then you'd phrase
it, "what made me smart." You with your
chi chi art, your interludes of lyric
boredom in which you lay about in your
elegant dress criticizing "the American
daytime tv," your Tunisian pal, likewise
disdainful, distributed upon the couch
in his Arabic finery.

Nietzsche would have approved
your patent for reordering life
and simultaneous passion for
your island of friends, the past,
childhood. Nothing comes without
pain, not cabin, summer house,
swinging rope, not secret hoard
buried in a sealed mason jar time
capsule. You grew serious, strove
to hold us close but couldn't
help going west again, knuckles
pale at the wheel of your buff
Corolla as you mounted Colorado.

I want to link up with you somewhere,
Toronto, Key West, not just talk to
you in stupid, elegiac tones. My plan was
to marry you from the time you were five
and us run off to beautiful Bend, Oregon,

or coastal Maine. Can't you rise from
your ashes, take wing like the grown
woman you are and you and me go fishing
and build a fire and cook those always
brainless bluegills? Wherever you are
I believe that matter's indestructible,
that creation reverses entropy and that
you remain splendid in your outrageous
dress, your plain words, your proud eye.

Maskmaker, you have
   become your disguise.
Have become appearances,
   fabrics, leather, paper,
images we see everywhere,
   sansara, the world, grief,
everything impermanent.
   We can touch you
just by reaching out.
   Go with us everywhere.

Margaret Crown

Shall I compare my grief, Margaret,
to tramping through *multiflora rose*
in the woods at the end of the orchard?
I want to. But you slipped away gradually,
Harold hand in hand with you in your extreme age,
died so peacefully, so beautifully,
courage and love in your counting down to heaven,
that no one shed tears at Farmington Methodist,
or after, when we planted Dogwood in your memory
behind the house on the brow of Crown Hill.

To view the coal outcrop along the creek back there
you must brave *multiflora*. The path
twists, dips, rises through red oak, red bud, hickory,
that was a road to the lost Civil War hill farms.
How Harold, then Gene, delighted to tell of it,
multiflora the panacea of the Conservation Service.
It wouldn't spread, they said. Nor choke, nor snag.
And all the time, darling Margaret, it crept among us,
tore, when we weren't looking, at our trouser legs,
our blouses—the backs of our hands—
and Harold and then Gene took the tractor and
    mowed there,
between the unkempt rows of apples and pears,
along the fence where the cows walked back to the
    barn,

Red, the dog, at their heels, clamorous at sunset.
An order Harold made which we treasured
as with a twist he palmed each apple he picked,
then rolled it into the baskets of our anticipation.

Grief hid his face, Margaret, in our contemplating,
plain, Methodist windows. You smiled to show you
    understood,
followed Harold where the road rose, turned into the
    farm,
stood hand in hand with him near the apple shed,
looking, you two, into one another's eyes—
into afternoon settling over the valley.

Season's End

At haul-out the naked hull.
Scrapes, blisters, flaking
paint, all exposed.

Out of her element
she seems to brood, becomes
monumental in her hidden
shapes revealed.

Where is her dreaming life?
And if she somehow survived
to the great dry age—would
the people guess how she was
meant in all her strength
to reach down afternoons to
islands at the fiery edge?

We empty her of her comforts:
bedding, books, instruments,
the last of the booze.

Best give galley
a scrub, wipe down the head;
into the v-berth with boom,
whisker and spinnaker poles:
resurrection's a century away

and no one can say what we'll
find—in that promised life
next April when the trump sounds
and the sun goes gold again

From
Hangdog
Reef

Port Stanley

Detroit River North to South

You are lacing your boots at the Windmill
Point Light and Lakeside Trailer Court where
the river slides out of Lake St. Clair.

You are mixing Manhattans at Peche Island
over on the Canadian side. An owl in
the last tree in Ontario winks once.

You are saving string on Belle Isle.
Your hair is perfect. You have tap danced
across the water from Hiram Walker's.

You are honing hatchets at Medusa Cement.
One look and they head for the hills. You
are a singer of sexy songs in downtown Windsor.

You are hoeing tomatoes at the Ren Cen and
Cobo Hall. Listen to someone who is sincere
and likewise wants to ravish you, today.

You are kissing boyfriends at the door of
the USPO. This is next to the Port of
Detroit, where you're tucking in your blouse.

You are ironing shirts in the middle of the
Ambassador Bridge. What's the difference?
It's Saturday, and traffic's backed up as it is.

You are loosening your belt at Northwest
Steamship, South Windsor. Meanwhile there are gulls
fishing in small boats and apricots in the sky.

You are scratching your sheepdog's ears
at Great Lakes Steel Division, National
Steel Corporation, pride of Zug Island.

You are changing film at Ontario Hydro and
have a room to paint in the chaste boutique of
Wyandotte Chemical, opposite Fighting Island.

You are pruning the rose of the fourth asteroid in
a blue tearoom on Grosse Ile. Brass violins serenade
Amherstburg and the Livingstone Channel.

You are pretending to listen to the deacon of
mallards at Detroit River Light in Lake Erie.
No one has free will. You are the seasons.

Port Sanilac

Here's this earth girl—she likes
to get her feet wet, too—standing
croisé at the edge of Huron, that is,
standing in the third position and inclined
to the right as if listening for
her boyfriend's hand at the screen door
with her arms rounded and slightly
advanced from the body to make safe harbor
for boats bashed by the big lake.

I ran into her just at dark.
And what kind of girl, what's her story?
Always lived in the same town—same house,
likes to look out at the ore boats,
favors barn dances, band concerts, picnics,
and, which I think is more important,
she is ample, lets you know you're welcome—
smiles, says hi, brushes her hair back, makes
fishing boats, cruisers, power and sail her own.

Although it was dark the attendants were
still on duty, said we'll take your lines,
skipper; would you like a berth tonight?
And they handed *Aneirin* along the dock,
helped with the bumpers and tied her fast—
and when the boat was shipshape (with town so
close), I walked out for pie and coffee,

and the owner talked about a pond on his place . . .
the water as cold and clear as . . . first light.

Standing *croisé* at the edge of Huron her
eyes are the color of flax flowers, her hair
is straw, she is not fully awakened, is always
becoming. I'm not saying evil is tripped there
or the town's perfect. Was there but a short time
(cast off at half-past six the next morning),
but Port Sanilac, with her lapped seawalls,
her timbered docks, draws to herself the sailor,
let him test the wind, let ride the dark wave.

Storm off Pointe aux Barques Light

The sudden shift. We'd turned in towards
Grindstone, were running, boom vanged out,
thinking in that light air to try the small
craft harbor—say, a mile and a half off—
when the wind turned north, hard, and the
waves built up. Too risky to go in; too much
foul water to sail it, and so, unromantic
turn, we motored around to Port Austin, storm
jib up to steady and help drive us through.
That was the prose of it, with an untried
but unflipped crew and rain coming down
in gathering dusk. How was it? The boat rose
on the diagonal as waves broke beneath;
we gave the tiller a twist, we sounded
the troughs. Were we nervous? Feeling harassed?
Enough already of this incidental blow?
Crests shining in the last light? But I say
it plainly, it is you—your dangers, your
sudden storms—I'd brave, for the sake of
clearing the mark just at dark and running
down into town—down the wind, down the backs
of waves into the calm knowledge of home.

Port Austin

INTO THE WET, BRIEF,
   GREEN AND WHITE
  FLASH OF WEEDS . . .
    —JOHN LOGAN 1923–1987

We put springlines on the boat to
keep the surge from banging it
into the pier, then I sent the two
crew to the bars to relax while I
cleaned up wet stuff, put boom

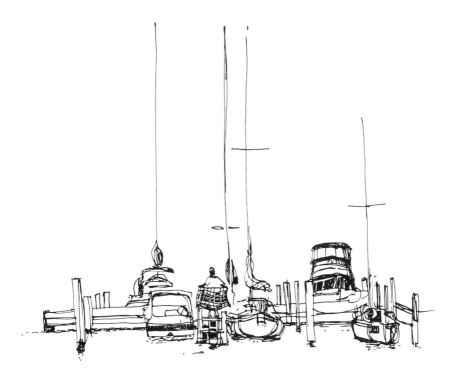

cover and boom tent on and, nursing
the last beer from the locker, sat
writing notes to myself: groceries,
fix-it list, log entry. The skipper
of the next boat to arrive told
me the front had surprised him,
too. It had been clear. The wind
did a one-eighty and gusted up.
We on our boat had been turning
into the approach to Grindstone.

Port Austin's building a new marina.
In two years they'll have hookups
for water and electric, an effective
seawall, better ways to tie up. This
is good. The locals could make a buck.

So we had to lay over a day—walked
up to Main Street, dined, played
pool, but then we got through to our
friend Ann—painter, printer, small
press quarterback and ex-big city girl,
who with husband and two kids had
moved operations north to the thumb.
Fine to be taken in hand by Ann, to
view her studio, lunch on homemade
soup and bread at her favorite dinette,
tour historic Grindstone City in that
ancient, roomy, rattling Pontiac wagon.

We'd have spent the blustery day
beering, banking shots, being bored
if it weren't for Ann and her pretty
face—Ann of the giant green, blue,
gray canvases of water and sky, Ann of
miniatures. I had had this urgent sense
that so much back at the boat needed
ordering, seeing to, planning. Busy
me. But to be treated to that elegant
studio and beautiful house transformed
the time and made everything whole.

Oscoda

Holding down the lake, one time,
by my lonesome, docked at Oscoda—
one strung-out landing along the river;
place stinks of fish guts, barbecue,
outboard motor oil—perfect for sports
fishers: trawlers, deep-rigs, one-day
charterers. Rain when I pulled in—
the people duck into the shop. Not
a grocery, not a bar on the road,

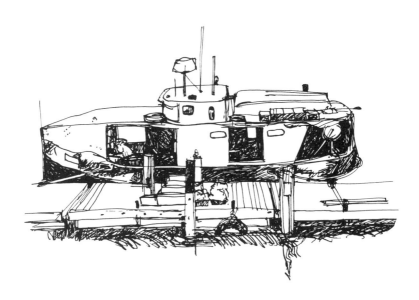

just rental slips and boat sales:
outdrive marine. I'm grousing,
fixing supper, holding my nose when
along about five it clears and the
big rigs take to the lake again.
People still-fish in john boats,
picnickers appear in the park.
Turns out the cigar-smoking old
guy in the three-story stinkboat
who's crowding my space wants to move.
We hustle lines, straighten him out—
I'm just zonking out when a guy yells
hey! It's a charter boat back;
they're at the tap, fishboard and
gutbucket lay out under the yard
light. They're offering me filet.
I accept and start cooking. Next
morning, early, the old guy's wife,
from the cruiser, hunts for their
dog. It's a cock-a-poo, not for boats,
ran off when she walked it. Oscoda,
you are kind and cruel with your
losses and dinners. I remember you well.

Alpena No Joke

Oh, you're really never happy
to enter or take my leave, but some
contrary wind or exasperating gale
or hot, unsettling calm troubles
all our hellos and good-byes. You are
a woman perfect in your imperfections,
an ordinary town writ large where
the streets are plain and the plantings
fail to protect from the sun, passionate
selves hidden by the sun, but when
the mariner leaps ashore at nightfall
and his steps bear him to the center,
past displays in windows, past shop
doors and on to the perpetually lit
crosswalks, Alpena, your loveliness
is the fire asmolder beneath and
beyond those unequal parts, embers
transcendent in a plain face, breast,
shoulder, groin—at once ablaze with
retributive anger and consuming desire.
We take one another to ourselves,
town of thunder. We have our way.

Presque Isle

Terns. Gulls. A wrecked wharf, rubble and timber.
Reefs crisscross the mouth of the shallow bay.

The state has plans for finger docks,
electric hookup, water, gas pumpout—

as if this small shelter were not enough.
But once, in the day of trapping, fishing,

lumber, land-rush, thick coastal traffic,
the place stank, groaned, chafed, grew pungent with
    trade.

What now, as there are condos down the way?
Still, at the Old Light House and Museum,

the rule is "Hands On," and when you hold the
ancient, brass telescope to your eye, you may

dimly discern the name on the bow of the
self-unloader passing inside the down-bound lane,

just as they used to. The keepers, man, wife,
a garrulous seventy, attend; his dad, too,

who was born in April of 'ninety-three.
They delay supper, urge us to ascend the snuffed

fieldstone lighthouse, to toll the bell that
once graced the Lansing city hall clock tower.

The sound makes our skull bones throb
bringing it back: loggers, trappers, boatmen,

that life of teeth, hair, nails, roots,
tree bark, fish knives, the sun westering—

that working the burnt land in all weathers.
Next morning some boats go north: Rogers City,

Cheboygan, the Straits; some south to Alpena,
Harrisville, Oscoda. We're last to leave.

Lens and keepers, they magnified what was.
Next time, we ourselves will have changed.

Listen to the gulls: how can it be otherwise.
Dredging, docks, lighting, ramp, and swim zone—

a new day. We wanted to hang on to the old,
the ruin in itself seemed so fragile.

Port Elgin to Tobermory

PETER FISHER, 1943–1983
PELICAN

1.

Everything nautical, says Jack,
Is built to fail—which lets you off
When you're not first to cross the line.

Jack has a brand new suit of sails,
Ergo, my seven-year-old rags
Confer on me the winning edge.

A cool rise. To make Little Tub
In time for drinks and dining out
We depart Port Elgin just at six.

Three other boats come out: Jack leads,
I'm next, the old guys in the Bayfield
Follow me. The port in the head

Leaks at the flange, I discover,
As waves we take over the bow
Flood side decks; the jib's overpowered,

And my seasick crew won't go below.
It's this broad reach, radios Jack,
All the way from here to Cape Hurd.

Who to switch jibs on the foredeck,
Who to make lunch and clear up, but me?
Who sponge up the cabin sole?

In a passage I was reading from
The Essays, the sage remarked, "truly,
Man is a marvelously vain,

Diverse, and undulating object."
Nonetheless we're holding our own
In a big wind on a longish run.

2.

At two we reach the mark, hand sails,
Cruise in along the line of buoys.
There is the wreck of the *Freedom*

Thirty-three, abraded hull and
Broken spar, on a steel yard trailer
In the city lot. Where we tie up

A work crew of young men (one nearly
Smashes his hand) fits long, lateral
Iron bolts into new dock sections,

And in the Bayside Doughnut Shop,
Where *Chi* and *Aneirin* swap lies,
A laughing Chinese girl peels paper

From the wall behind the counter.
Always a race, Jack says. Always
Have something wrong in case you lose.

So Tobermory cooks in the sun
And the later boats can't find space.
You came ashore at Flowerpot Island

Who were committed to the deep
And boisterous wave. Four years you'd run
The lake-long single-handers race

Out of Cheboygan, and today,
Beneath the waning strawberry moon,
You'd crossed the line alone.

North of the Blue Water Bridge

Big lake, I can, I know, talk to
you all day—you don't "hear" or
"sense" what I'm saying; don't
have the faculty of "caring"; you
are not "sentient" in the least—

so you are the perfect listener.
One time, north of Kincardine,
a bird hitched a ride with me:
a message, possibly, but, more
likely, a bird hitching a ride.

Coming up under the bridge into
you, Huron, at Sarnia, the first
time was the same as entering an
ocean. But that's not true now. I
cannot love the finite with that

infinite love I'd saved for the
ideal. I know you too well. Still
you, as lake, have supported so
much that is lucky, grand, secret,
trivial, useful or failed that

it's history. One of these days
I'll go off with my pocket change
and you will flood the same. I'll

sail past Goderich and Port Elgin
and head over towards Great Duck

Island—which is, I've always assumed,
of no interest. Why go down there?
I don't know. Your ability to be
yourself, it could be. You are merely
a great lake and refuse to do more.

A History of St. Ignace

TEACH US, GOOD LORD, TO SERVE
THEE AS THOU DESERVEST . . .
—LOYOLA

1. the reformation of character

Before the flood we lived here
as on an island, not easily but
with our trials of time and distance
through these staked and stone-daft
waters. No otherness made us
change the ways we saw ourselves.
Some said we feared to enter in
lest our island should sink into
the Straits, but the cove you call
East Moran Bay gentled our canoes.
Bluffs rose to declarations of stars,
and those come down from the lakehead
held their own in the long consultations,
dogs barking in the willowy darkness
beyond the circle of light.

2. the alignment

Twice hourly the wake of Mackinac
ferries jostles vessels docked at
the city marina. Down State Street
crowds tour the shops for pastel

postcards, painted porcelain,
printed placemats, and petite Indian
maidens in buckskins and dyed feathers
paddling miniature canoes. The depot's
a stunned, street-level bomb shelter,
schedule crayoned to the wall:
"bus south passing through five A.M."

3. *the strengthening*

We no sooner condemn this town than we
make much of savages. The fault divides
the Straits and splits the bluffs.
Brace me in my weakness. Nowadays
I cannot find You to whom in my despair
I've pledged myself, though You stand
beside me. I too am implicated in
the obscure crime for which the surrogate
sun makes miserably humid the shops,
the parking, the dark graves of
heroes ringed with an iron pale.

4. *the transformation*

I would achieve an animal redemption
in the flesh, would couple with You
in her. I'd seal and bond with her,
betray that sensible other in myself
which holds back violence—though we

may not become the people we were,
may no longer, at the crossing of trails,
rekindle the fires in our bones or
track our bright shadows into the light.
Lord, create in us changed lives—
even as we drink deep, and thirst,
and drink again—whatever the cost.

Mackinaw City to Beaver Island

Curve under the bridge,
  sail upwind
    to Grays Reef Passage,
negotiate the channel,
  beat west
    to St. James Bay.
A day trip.
  What can you see?
    From St. Ignace to Brevort
the north shore;
  Waugoshance Point
    to the south;
the abandoned lighthouse,
  the working lighthouse,
    and, as the afternoon wanes,
Hog Island,
  Garden Island,
    Beaver Island itself.
These are the deck-visible,
  these you'd sketch
    in your careful periplum—
a kind of strip chart
  you make when you traverse
    new ground:

it shows all you can see
  on either hand
    to the horizon.
Beyond that strip,
  beyond islands,
    distant mainland,
birds,
  the water snake you saw swimming
    miles offshore,
lies terra incognita,
  the here-be-dragons,
    lake-of-fire,

edge-of-the-world
  falling off place,
    the known unknown.
Perhaps some native
  with large gestures,
    tries to teach you
the lay of that hidden land
  speaking a throttled tongue
    deep into midnight.
Or you hold in your hand
  some few dissolving pages:
    the last notes
of the navigator No-man,
  burned out,
    his burned record
or stone tablet:
  runes, symbols, ogham
    unearthed at burial sites:
weed, stars, birds, fish
  that led him out, led him back
    the first and last to go there.
A line of clouds,
  cumulus humilis,
    marches to the south.
The sun westering
  traps your eye,
    the wind abates.

And the further you go,
　　the more you breach
　　　　the unknown—
with its trackless beaches,
　　beasts unafraid,
　　　　silences—
the less you know;
　　beyond dragons,
　　　　fire lakes,
beyond the misty edge,
　　when you have left it behind
　　　　and stand
in the unearthly light
　　alone as Adam,
　　　　chilled, struck dumb,
there lies space,
　　larger than it was,
　　　　curved back upon itself,
serpent, tortoise writ large,
　　sidereal,
　　　　and you, astonished,
unable to see back beyond the hills,
　　sketching, plotting,
　　　　remeasuring the way you have come.

Crossing Lake Michigan

There was no one
  out there
    in the middle
so I set the autopilot,
  went below for a nap—
    such a gray day,
wind ten to twelve,
  no one in sight.
    Lucky me.
Dozed,
  woke up,
    watched a fly
parading upside down
  on the cabin liner, then
    got up and looked out.
Oreboat half a mile north.
  Funny,
    no one on deck,
no one
  visible
    in the pilot house—
I had to stop,
  turn upwind to
    avoid him—not

a sound, not a
    soul, but just
        this big burnt-orange guy
with the blank windows
    sliding by—did he
        spot me
or did he
    sail on south blind
        as the sky closed in?

South Manitou Island

At the Visitor's Center trail maps showed
Where you could hike and what the distance was
From point to point: this last I overlooked
And set off for the Valley of the Giants
With no food or water or insect rub
Ignorant how far the place would be.
Walked and walked, and still kept trudging
Till after seven miles the road ran out
And I found myself in a stand of large trees—

The timbermen who'd logged off the forest
Somehow missed this far nub of the island.
Some old white cedars had survived by chance.
I'd passed, in the heat of day, stunned farm-
   steads,
Orchards mobbed with thickets of juniper,
Woodlots a tangle of dusty, second growth,
But here the air was damp, cool, smelt of pitch,
Drifted green on the eyes, snapped in the lung:
This one small stand that not so long ago
Stretched across—much of the upper Midwest.

Hiked back to the beach thirsty and fatigued,
Then, as the museum closed its doors at two,
Stood gazing at oil lamps, old jars, pitchforks,
Faded snapshots, records of record crops,

STILL   Ann Mikolowski

Quilts, foot-warmers, hand-carved salt boxes,
    churns.
What a comeuppance, to sail across the lake
Expecting I'd find the Great Spirit's house.
The truth was something else: a light station,
A woodlot for steamers, farmsteads where
Pious Germans had raised prize rye crops—
And now neither lens nor plow nor broadax
Served, and so it had become National
Lakeshore, which Uncle Sam planned to restore.

But if you were merely cruising Michigan
It made a good place to put in. And the dunes,
They demanded respect. There were warnings to

Stay on the trail, there was nothing to drink,
Climbing them was strenuous, heart stopping,
Wet snow avalanched down them easily,
You could lose your footing in their always
Shifting sands, only to surface, bone dry,
Years down the line, in the image of a tree:
One of those ghost forest snags that had suc-
    cumbed,
Green-shouldered, to the blown depths, and rose,
In our own day, as from the lake bed,
Leafless, cold as stone, beseeching heaven.

At Leland

Just outside the harbor entrance
house-size stinkboat passes at
speed. I've seen him coming and
go hard over on the tiller. He
veers, then looks back, astonished.
His wake hits. I can see his wife,
there on the bridge, looking at
him—this benign, comfortable,
prosperous, middle-aged man. If
the son-of-a-bitch met you at lunch,
in church, at work, or just walking
along, he wouldn't dream of
knocking you down—or would he?

Blind River to Meldrum Bay

1.

Noon, the twenty-mile crossing in fog,
Not sailing out of need but wanting
A move, a look of the sort the town
Could not show with its ruined mill,
The bridge, and the impounded river.
After an interval, Mississagi Island
Thinly apparent in the mist, gulls
Stopped upon slack Dog Point Shoal,
And beyond Mississagi a windshift;
Though you rose to the lifts you were headed,
Let to drift as the air fell off.
Fog that would not resolve but lightened
And darkened, promised and took away.

I would walk with you in the city park
Where the sun itself gives life to the
Ancient drift of snow-melt and townlife.
No one's perfect. No one can match

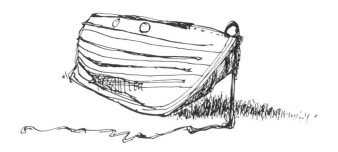

Your pride, your valor, your gray and
Unforgiving eye. Here in mid-channel,
We negotiate, as an act of will, these
Mists, this loss and unbecoming weave,
Love and not-love scoring the hand.

2.

By the wish to reach dock, benchmark,
Brass set in stone, point fixed by
Surveyors to all other known points,
Will work all afternoon through
Wave and clouddrift until at last
Batture Island with its own flashing light
Shows low, dark in the south, then bluffs
Beyond, then the buoy and, finally, the town.
I did not leave you, ever: we crossed
Together, though you stood in your dooryard
Tending stubbornly to gate, garden, house
That you own, that no one can ever take.

Pasture, and the one hill with pine trees.
We have looked into depths, hand in hand,
Tested cold places where swimmers numb and
Slip away though they are buoyant as fish:
This lake wetness deepening to aqua,
Ledge below ledge the sun receding until,
In our own waking darkness, we were joined,
Were the imagined pictures stars construe
In their brief and accidental choreography.

Aird Island

On the chart, a daybeacon, but fresh growth
must have obscured it. We found the entrance,
turned in, and anchored without seeing it:

an orange triangle on a high post
or fixed by a steel frame to a rock face.
The rule is, the marker stands in the clear:

the light strikes the eye, which acquaints the
   brain,
which, expecting it, recognizes it—
but this takes me out of my depth. The hand

takes the boat into the cove on its own—
on its own, for our purposes, connects,
communes with the object, and takes us in.

What more did those mad philosophers want?
I caught a bass in the reed beds. We cleaned,
cooked, and ate it along with meat, salad,

soup, and toast. We were happy with the path
of it. Wine too, and cake that we had on board.
But none of us knew what we did when we

took bites with our forks: how did *that*
choice come about—which cause impelled which
word? And we jabbered all through the dishes.

Mike and Tamra camped in the cockpit,
sleeping bags, gloves, and caps against the cold,
binoculars to find constellations—

a star wheel, an almanac of the skies.
What do we know? Orion, possibly,
or the spun fires of Cygnus, the swan.

How do we navigate if not by faith?
Staring down the night this exuberant
doubt, whether or not we are truly "there."

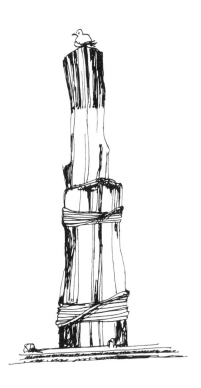

Picnic on the Heights of Croker Island

A gull wanted lunch.
An elderly, unkempt bird,
big, too, and, in the way he stared,
judgmental.
He landed on bare rock
just where we sat, stood there,
wouldn't budge.
The others circled, complained,
younger, glossier,
some in the air below our peak,
some on our level.
Blue water, blue sky, clouds, islands.
The small grasses in the crevices dry
as there had been little rainfall.

This is your turf, grandfather gull,
but scram. We're not hosting you,
or your pals,
though you and yours
follow us to Burnt Island Bank
and on south
and out of the channel.

Hangdog Reef

Small Craft Channel, Georgian Bay

To love you is to attempt Hangdog Reef.
The day before, a cruiser strikes rock.
So easily: yards off course, and granite,
Just below the surface, his rudder smashed.
Later on, fog, and it's hard to see buoys
Among bays, passages and island groups—
Simple on the charts, but wait and see.
I anchor in an ear of rock and trees.
Darkness descends. Something wants to be born
That wings across the lakes from your small
   house
And I'm so alone the sound of your latch
Makes me sit up. The boat swings on its hook.
I button up, douse lights, am drifting off
When you open the door and ask me in.

Next morning, wide Shawanaga Inlet
And Turning Island. Brisk air, west-southwest,
The sky dark with promise of rain: I take
A spar on the wrong side but turn in time.
This is no way to learn to be myself,
But you yourself have gone on more than once
When the weather was not to your liking.
Middle channel west to Sedgewick Point, then

Through the passage at Pointe au Baril
And around Nares Ledges to Shoal Narrows,
Leith Island, and so west to open water.

This the approach to Hangdog Reef. And here's
My metaphor, because this is the place,
And this the sort of wild and windy day
Seas build offshore and break in the passage
And you have to ask yourself why this way?
The channel skirts outward-trending strata,
Then doubles back. Waves obscure the markers—
Even then, when you've seen them through the
   wet,
There are, worse luck, rock intrusions to clear.
I'm clutching the chart, gripping the tiller,
Straining to see over the cabin top . . .
An elderly couple I met later at Britt
Told me they took their steel-hulled trawler
   through
Years ago, before the channel was buoyed.
But then I'm talking about you and me,
How, when the wind's up one of us falls off,
Misreads the water, gybes violently,
Bangs heads with the lithic gods of lakes,
And though we are in love and do love well,
That reef will test us as long as we breathe,
And the next time, and the time after, too.
Place names fascinate me. Look at the charts.
As in sheltered Alexander Passage,

Cow, Elm Tree, Meneilly, Miniwabin,
Jean, Bushy and Choctaw Islands. From there,
A run of nine miles through shallows and
   troughs.
The air grievous, and me wondering whether
I truly know to be out in this mess.
Beyond McNab Rocks I can force the boat
No farther into the wind and fall back
Into Byng Inlet. Wing on wing upstream,
It's half an hour to Wright's Marine, in Britt,
Where, after a parley in the boat store
I'm assigned a slip with electricity
And helped to it by a t-shirted young man
Who goes round and takes my lines.
And it's only three when the boat's docked,
And calm here out of the reach of the lake
And warm in this narrow place, but still I am
Spaced, slow on my feet, as if I'd just now
Learned to use my brain. Time to clean up,
Make sense of tangles of line, wet sails,
Soggy charts. This is the way the sun
Breaks through, lights us into the ordinary:
And we are the same, the two of us,
In our former selves, in our despair,
And we are not the same, are transformed,
Have become winged, have risen beyond reason,
And no force will ever divide us
Though our own houses conspire against us,
Though we forsake one another tomorrow.

The Bustards

1.

In my wishful future you
follow me into the Bustards,

that cluster of island states,
principalities, possessions.

I'm lying under a pine tree.
You canoe towards me, unseen

as the sun walks west into
the first days of harvest.

2.

We bed in the pine needles.
Beneath us, the granite

struggles to hold on. It
floats in the magma of doubt.

Of all the islands, no two
speak civilly, but will whisper

through the long night
because the dark relieves them.

3.

When we take ship and sail
our doubled selves will remain,

marooned, winter-starved, chilled
so that the hands and faces sting.

The stone's gray, patched green
with lichens, dark with the

afterspeech of glaciers. We'll
live here as we breathed, engage,

become immersed, imprint our cells
in these ancient strata.

Mathematics

How can the pure world of numbers
correspond to the green turbulence
and rock smash of waters in their
gull-sung and accidental distances?
Yet we compute courses by degrees,
progress by hours elapsed, location
by triangulation. What other link
do we have between mind and matter
proves so true that we may share
accurate travel with one another—
point to point? It's as if you and I
navigated perfectly each on a watch
while the other read or slept or
prepared a meal, so well did we know
one another's calculus. Yes, true—
storms, compass anomalies, uncharted
currents may throw us off—nothing
is free of danger. But that too,
with care, we may prefigure. However
fierce the hurt we suffer, we may,
if we will, survive and prosper.

A Tour of Flowerpot Island

Beachy Cove's the social center.
The lighthouse is lonely as hell.
The snakes have no natural enemies.

This island, with its campsites,
nature trails, cave, marl bed,
boat landing—it's closed down
winters, the lighthouse too, as
the lake itself's frozen tight.

The four of us hiked it and on
the beach picnicked. In my
childish head I propose that the
island itself has taken snapshots:
us special trekkers. And that
during the long winter silence
it thumbs through its album,
chuckles, perhaps—unbelieving—
at our all too usual high jinks.

This isn't really winter silence.
In the grassy places beneath
trees, among roots, sheltered by
overhangs, the secret lives of
the place go on. Birds, marmots,
insects even, though the snakes

sleep soundly enough in their
hideaways, delicate tongues stilled.

The three levels of ecology,
they're in no way subsumed to
the season. From the forested
boreal heights through the
deciduous foreshore down to the
shoreline itself you descend as
in a continual fall towards the
great sleep of the lake. And
to think how we surfed our boat
downwind from Cove Island to
arrive in time for an expedition
to the top.

      I lie down in the
mixture of fine mud and the
shells of mollusks, my marl bed
and winter hibernating place.
Sure it's cold. First in my back
and arms and groin: painful. I
shake a little. But you can't
just walk. Can't just be sentimental
and go. Better to stay in place,
hurting, and get on with winter.

Depth Sounder

Scans silently,
   flickers spider digits,
      denotes decimal depths.

Why aren't we all so equipped,
   sensors in our shoes,
      monitor strapped to chest?

Look, a reef dead ahead:
   you might have seen green shapes,
      gray knees of granite,

Might have recognized temptation,
   greed, avarice, envy,
      but had not been warned.

Not a thud,
   not a blow that's cushioned,
      but a loud, hard bang.

The engine's whipped off its mounts,
   the hull's stressed,
      the rudder's torn away,

Drinks spill,
   the boom gybes,
      your guests look confused.

Hours later, a large, plastic stinkboat
   rips out your king post,
      trying too hard to set you free.

I mean evil,
   a sounder that can spot pride
      and warn you in time.

Don't go, stay home
   if you can't put together
      depth and location.

Although, I'll admit,
   there are places so deep
      the readout stays blank:

Lie back, relax, you deserve it,
   good sail—quite safe,
      suspended between heaven and hell.

Anchor

1. The boat:

a ribbed house,
unto itself an all.

2. The water: stem cracker

and rainbow maker, deep beyond
sounding or shallow to ground you.

3. The ground:

marl's not uncommon,
mud's deep, look for gravel

inshore, boulders near
ledges where
granite's upthrust.

I dig in: the harder
the haul on the rope
the deeper I bite.

4. The shore:

you must know whether
windshifts might trap you—

Must assure you'd not tangle,
foul prop,
lose tackle to others.

Must opt to cleat bow or
stern first, set one
line or two, tie to a tree.

5. How speak to this topic,

how grip, submerged,
the unseen bottom,

sand, sediment, loose stones, muck,
loss and sunk brass—
and the ware, how can it hold:

swivels, eye and jaw end;
shackles twisted and flat;
quick links, lap links?

My science eludes. I am
kin to laws, logic itself,
that seem iron, but may lift and let go.

Change of Weather: Spring

That the flesh of us should respond
to pressure: suddenly we're zooming,
bow wave, quarter wave, rail down,
without cause, final, formal, efficient,
but the light's golden and we go fast
where before we stood, not in the mood.

Somewhere the anatomy for it: a sensor
connects to a valve, switches on discrete
circulation—infusion, penetrates cell
to marrow, dermis, tip of cilia, all—
it's as if we were crafted to fly free
before the rise of the moon, to answer

to advent of starlight, soar to predawn
falselight, browse freely in the good
half-darkness before the sun appears.
The season's a cue, where at equinox
we'll scrape, sand, caulk, paint, set
to rights cockpit, cabin, rig and gear,

ice gone from open and blown bay,
ice-melt in streams, ice chunks downriver,
ice rows slow to disperse from beaches
but gone at last. Mud fields steaming, wind
blowing blue, the older willows crackling,
branch blown down, whitecap on lake.

The naked elemental hand caresses the
inmost tissue—the sensitive, pastel
or violently shaded surface, root and
sexual stem, visceral keel and sprawled,
sinuous nerve strand. We stretch, punch
through the surface. The glacier's gone.

One more year. A gift, a life given to
launch, step, tune, make sail. Clearly
we do not think too little, any of us, but
to go as if propelled by an argument of
air, curving steady at the angle, sucked
past the main, heeling against the force.

Ship Castle

In the deep ship castle of my head
the two of us cross through. Sea birds
and fat trout and messenger eels—
we go to school to them. Each of our
limbs they prompt—here a deft peck,
there a nudge with a nose, now a tail
tug—to teach us passionate embraces,
love desperate to be joined in our
fighting across and weathering home.

Salons in each of the cardinal points.
Views north, a bay east where waking
you may, in your beamy berth, suffer
sun nakedness because the dawn loosens
each and every spun garment so that
lovers, opening eyes, have no choice
but to turn to one another once more—
heeling to the wind, my ship castle,
this while, footing it, running fast.

To this palely glittering winter noon
a vessel passing. The river's ice,
the bay's a snowy, insurmountable plane.
We store our gear in the cabin below,
let go the lines, move off from the
land. How is it, if we were not taught,

that each knows to haul in or adjust

blocks, or to turn up into it, if not

that we have learned in such a ship castle?

Cuisine

Take me. Breakfast is eggs
I've boiled, a dozen in advance;
cold cereal often with canned milk;
coffee and juice—everything taken
fast while I scribble notes to
myself.

    Lunch: apple, nectarine,
or, late in the season, a pear;
a cheese or peanut butter and jelly
or salami sandwich; chocolate chip
cookies; coffee from the thermos
or Pepsi.

    Supper's one pot, one dish:
rice in a bag; canned pressed chicken,
say; cut up and add onion, green pepper,
tomato; pour in a can of chicken soup
for stock and add any more spices you
have on board—if you've got white wine
add half a cup. After six nights in a
row, however, this dish may have lost
piquancy.

    Now take my friend Aileen. No
"boat food" cook she. She'll have a
bag of potatoes in her galley, a pound

of ground round, canned peas, and pie.
Or she'll have pork chops and will cut
up the potatoes and make french fries
or cream the potatoes using flour, or make
gravy. Her husband, Jack, expects this
on their boat.

Last year I had some gourmet
cooks on board mine. We had five-course
dinners: hors d'oeuvres, soup, freshly caught
(by me) fish, grain-fed beef, canned corn,
salad, and chocolate chip cookies for dessert.
This was my best crew ever.

Quaintest dinner?
I made my nephew Kevin take a turn. He
served warmed up canned chicken stuffing
on paper dinnerware, soup, jug wine, and
a salad consisting of a ring of Ritz crackers
(also on paper dinnerware) centered around
a radish. For each of us.

My one disaster was
assisted by an act of God. We were docked at
Scudder, Pelee Island, and I'd invited Jack and
Aileen over for my usual: glop. Sustained high
winds and swells on the lake caused a bad surge

in the harbor. We'd no more sat down and had me
serve the glop up than Aileen turned green
and fled.

Scuba

Divers, walking the River St. Clair.
What a story. Snagged lures, wrecks,
drowned bodies—items you'd liken to
objects or images in the hidden mind.

The hulls of ships passing overhead;
the surface itself; above and beyond
the surface the blue inconstant light—
it's the true heaven or "here below."

At Big Tub, Tobermory, through the
ice, they walk the bottom Januaries.
It's transitive. You say, "let's us
dive that wreck." Likewise, it's cold.

But wet suits warm them. Thicknesses
of sponge rubber so like the layers
seals, whales, sea lions have. Moon
creatures in wet suit, mask, flippers.

Down under we're something else. All
anxieties dissolve. Time slows down.
We breathe deep in an atmosphere of
shells and rippled sand, and nothing

in the world we've left behind—
unworthy deeds, ice storms, promises,
stress—can touch us, now that
we've come to terms with the deep.

After Christening

St. Mary's in Greektown, Detroit

To Alexandra, daughter of Michael and Diane,
we bring a small gift. She is three weeks old,

who huddles against the flowered sheet in her
   crib
with the sleep of rivers, silent and deep, that

in spring will unlock and let live the beamy
   equinox,
secret of root and branch, truth winged from the
   nest.

Ice-melt and snow-melt, the quickening of
   streams,
these sing in your drowsing sigh, your brief,
   sweet breaths.

Then we wake you, you've slept past your feeding:
your blue, your troubled, impatient eye

takes us in, uncomprehending, slowly wakening.
Alexandra, we welcome you to the moving world,

to the dip and sky-hurl of swing sets, to
that far, weightless moment at the top of the arc,

alike, when your father will toss you high
and you know to land safe in his two strong arms

clinging to the center and drawn from that center
till the world itself turns and you can no more.

Factories along the River

The "thereness" of you—seen from
a distance—that pleasing, happy,
foolish, aesthetic, philosophical
perspective of you that we can adopt
as long as we're not employees.

I mean you, Mister Detroit Edison
on the River St. Clair. And you,
Wyandotte Chemical, downriver from
Motor City, though you are now
torn down. And you, Medusa Cement.

That is to say, you have the
blank, monumental air of cathedrals,
museums, opera houses, state
capitals, though you're merely
a steel works or power plant.

I cite Uniroyal Tire, that was
west of the Belle Isle Bridge. *Ubi
sunt?* And the elegant Imperial Oil
Limited, at Sarnia with its Gothic
cracking towers and perpetual flame.

Perhaps it's that motoring upstream
it takes us so long to pass you by.
We're often drawn in towards you by

wind or current or by the strategy of
cutting corners where the river bends.

Think of words we associate with you:
industry, enterprise, manufacture; yet
you transcend language—we ourselves, it
is, with all our stepping back, who fall to
"weather," "fatigue," "hunger," "loss of self."

You're the stuff of sidings, tramways,
welded or riveted steel, slag ablaze,
mounted cranes, blow offs, conveyors
patiently edging coal, limestone, salt,
sand, taconite into conical tips.

To you, bulk cargo vessels—ore and
aggregate carriers, tankers, barges,
scrappers, grain boats, traders in
gypsum—are creatures of use, so many
watertight sleds, carts, hand trucks.

In our greed for words we take to
ourselves what we mistake for your
speech. We will not learn our own,
though the light on the river changes,
and you recede even as we approach.

Put-In-Bay

I'm asking you with your blue notes
and sky high C's, let's get rid of
the riffraff. No more stereos blasting
through the anchorage and along the
docks all night long.

Let's burn the bars with their bad
pizza and barfing twenty-year-olds.

And the vulgar, middle-aged couples
in their four-story motor yachts
who look neither right nor left but
capsize small craft in their wakes,
let them tie up and watch their TVs
elsewhere.

Don't forget the cadre of racers,
competitive, intolerant, uniformly
arrogant in their sleek, expensive
sloops—let's post them to Cleveland.

Let's raft off together civilly,
uncomplaining, wrapped in one another's
lines. It's our own fault. My thief,
my felon: we have met the enemy and
he is us.

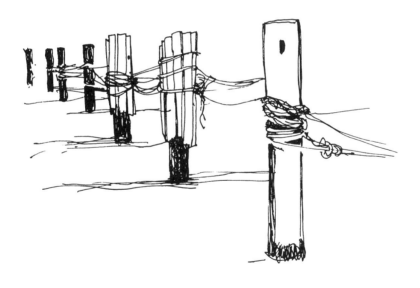

Winter Storage

The boat's cradled, cold-proofed,
high, dry in the yard at Erieau.

I take a half day off from work,
drive down, check the tarp.

It's the shortest day of the year,
but mild. Wind blows off the lake.

Somehow the bilge has got full of
water. I've got to caulk topsides.

There is so much to fix or pay for.
This is the year boats fall apart.

My friend Jack helps me take off
some equipment—the brass clock,

which we unscrew from the bulkhead,
a gimballed lamp, tools, a radio.

It's dank inside: sponges, buckets,
bumpers, line, stuff strewn around.

No one, meaning me, gave it a good
cleaning. Still, I feel a rush.

I love my boat, I tell Jack. I love
being here. Wind has shredded the

tarp. We untie it, fold it, toss it
in the car. From now on the days will

lengthen as if they were lined up in
a patient row of boats waiting it out.

Kincardine

Agawa Rock

Birds, wind, water. Would it become
an island kingdom if it could—

wooded, rich in fauna, peopled
by makers of song? One day, say,

a ship drops anchor in the cove.
The crew comes ashore in a boat.

The natives lead them up a trail
to the naked, original rock.

The air is thin, they are so high.
All the islands lie at their feet.

The blue lake rises around them like
sides of a blue, enameled saucer.

At last the day of parting arrives.
The rock makes way, sees them down the

trail to the beach. They board the ship,
which returns them to the mainland far

to the south. And the singers, changed
into birds, their words become the

lament of streams. Lodges and trails
disappear. Only the figures remain,

angular in ochre and bear grease,
flat on the face of the rock—

except them there is no one here:
carved granite, birds, wind, water.

Titles in the
Great Lakes Books Series

Deep Woods Frontier: A History of Logging in Northern Michigan, by Theodore J. Karamanski, 1989

Orvie, The Dictator of Dearborn, by David L. Good, 1989

Seasons of Grace: A History of the Catholic Archdiocese of Detroit, by Leslie Woodcock Tentler, 1990

The Pottery of John Foster: Form and Meaning, by Gordon and Elizabeth Orear, 1990

The Diary of Bishop Frederic Baraga: First Bishop of Marquette, Michigan, edited by Regis M. Walling and Rev. N. Daniel Rupp, 1990

Walnut Pickles and Watermelon Cake: A Century of Michigan Cooking, by Larry B. Massie and Priscilla Massie, 1990

The Making of Michigan, 1820-1860: A Pioneer Anthology, edited by Justin L. Kestenbaum, 1990

America's Favorite Homes: A Guide to Popular Early Twentieth-Century Homes, by Robert Schweitzer and Michael W. R. Davis, 1990

Beyond the Model T: The Other Ventures of Henry Ford, by Ford R. Bryan, 1990

Life after the Line, by Josie Kearns, 1990

Michigan Lumbertowns: Lumbermen and Laborers in Saginaw, Bay City, and Muskegon, 1870-1905, by Jeremy W. Kilar, 1990

Detroit Kids Catalog: The Hometown Tourist, by Ellyce Field, 1990

Waiting for the News, by Leo Litwak, 1990 (reprint)

Detroit Perspectives, edited by Wilma Wood Henrickson, 1991

Life on the Great Lakes: A Wheelsman's Story, by Fred W. Dutton, edited by William Donohue Ellis, 1991

Copper Country Journal: The Diary of Schoolmaster Henry Hobart, 1863-1864, by Henry Hobart, edited by Philip P. Mason, 1991

John Jacob Astor: Business and Finance in the Early Republic, by John Denis Haeger, 1991

Survival and Regeneration: Detroit's American Indian Community, by Edmund J. Danziger, Jr., 1991

Steamboats and Sailors of the Great Lakes, by Mark L. Thompson, 1991

Cobb Would Have Caught It: The Golden Years of Baseball in Detroit, by Richard Bak, 1991

Michigan in Literature, by Clarence Andrews, 1992

Under the Influence of Water: Poems, Essays, and Stories, by Michael Delp, 1992

The Country Kitchen, by Della T. Lutes, 1992 (reprint)

The Making of a Mining District: Keweenaw Native Copper 1500-1870, by David J. Krause, 1992

Kids Catalog of Michigan Adventures, by Ellyce Field, 1993

Henry's Lieutenants, by Ford R. Bryan, 1993

Historic Highway Bridges of Michigan, by Charles K. Hyde, 1993

Lake Erie and Lake St. Clair Handbook, by Stanley J. Bolsenga and Charles E. Herndendorf, 1993

Queen of the Lakes, by Mark Thompson, 1994

Iron Fleet: The Great Lakes in World War II, by George J. Joachim, 1994

Turkey Stearnes and the Detroit Stars: The Negro Leagues in Detroit, 1919-1933, by Richard Bak, 1994

Pontiac and the Indian Uprising, by Howard H. Peckham, 1994 (reprint)

Charting the Inland Seas: A History of the U.S. Lake Survey, by Arthur M. Woodford, 1994 (reprint)

Ojibwa Narratives of Charles and Charlotte Kawbawgam and Jacques LePique, 1893-1895. Recorded with Notes by Homer H. Kidder, edited by Arthur P. Bourgeois, 1994, co-published with the Marquette County Historical Society

Strangers and Sojourners: A History of Michigan's Keweenaw Peninsula, by Arthur W. Thurner, 1994

Win Some, Lose Some: G. Mennen Williams and the New Democrats, by Helen Washburn Berthelot, 1995

Sarkis, by Gordon and Elizabeth Orear, 1995

The Northern Lights: Lighthouses of the Upper Great Lakes, by Charles K. Hyde, 1995 (reprint)

Kids Catalog of Michigan Adventures, second edition, by Ellyce Field, 1995

Rumrunning and the Roaring Twenties: Prohibition on the Michigan-Ontario Waterway, by Philip P. Mason, 1995

In the Wilderness with the Red Indians, by E. R. Baierlein, translated by Anita Z. Boldt, edited by Harold W. Moll, 1996

Elmwood Endures: History of a Detroit Cemetery, by Michael Franck, 1996

Master of Precision: Henry M. Leland, by Mrs. Wilfred C. Leland with Minnie Dubbs Millbrook, 1996 (reprint)

Haul-Out: New and Selected Poems, by Stephen Tudor, 1996

.